MURDER
BALLADS

Author Photo: Kevin Andre Elliott and Jake Adam York

Cover Art: *The Murder* by Paul Cezanne, 1868.
Used courtesy of the Walker Art Gallery, Liverpool, England

Book Design: Joel A. Bass

ISBN: 1-932418-15-6

Elixir Press
PO Box 27029
Denver, Colorado 80227

www.ElixirPress.com

Elixir Press is a nonprofit literary organization.

MURDER BALLADS

Jake Adam York

ELIXIR PRESS

for those who clear the thicket

Acknowledgments

Grateful acknowledgment and thanks to the editors of the following journals who have given these poems a hearing:

Blackbird, "Bunk Richardson," "Consolation," "On Tallasseehatchee Creek," and "Vigil"; *Brilliant Corners*, "In the Magic City"; *Cold Mountain Review*, "Release"; *Controlled Burn*, "Run On"; *Cross Roads*, "At Cornwall Furnace"; *DIAGRAM*, "Elegy for James Knox"; *Greensboro Review*, "Interferometry"; *Gulf Coast*, "Blood"; *H_NGM_N*, "Doppler," "Fell," "Under," and "What You Wish For"; *Louisiana Literature*, "Cannon" and "Looking for Cane Creek Furnace"; *New Orleans Review*, "Hush"; *Poetry Daily*, "Interferometry"; *Quarterly West*, "Negatives"; *Shenandoah*, "Walt Whitman in Alabama"; *The Southern Review*, "As Water" and "Janney"; *Texas Review*, "Iron"; *Third Coast*, "Descendant," "George Wallace at the Crossroads," and "Midnight, Furnace, Wind"; *Typo*, "Radiotherapy"

Thanks as well to the editors of *DIAGRAM* and *Blackbird* for nominating "Elegy for James Knox" and "Vigil" for Pushcart Prizes, to the judges of the 2004 Campbell Corner Poetry Prize for naming "Elegy for James Knox," "Vigil," and "Negatives" runners-up, and to Thom Tammaro for including "Walt Whitman in Alabama" in *Visiting Walt: Poems Inspired by the Life and Work of Walt Whitman* (University of Iowa Press, 2003).

Grateful acknowledgment and thanks as well to the Colorado Council on the Arts and the Sewanee Writers Conference for crucial support and challenge.

Unending thanks to my mentors, friends, and family—readers all —who have helped this work along, especially to my wife, without whom nothing.

Introduction

The Eliot of "Preludes" was haunted by specters, by trace deposits of the past in the present, finding himself moved by mundane images—morning crowds shuffling to coffee stands, fingers stuffing pipes, roving eyes of passersby, the imagined footsteps of long-gone generations—to apprehend the indelible impression of "some infinitely gentle/infinitely suffering thing." This same sensibility is found in Jake Adam York's *Murder Ballads*, a first book of moral intelligence and surprising beauty, a collection for which remembering is an inherently political act.

A Southerner by birth and temperament, York is distinctly attuned to questions of inheritance: our relation to the land and to the law, to justice done and undone. Everywhere the poet looks, relics turn up, charged texts and grisly histories: photographs of lynchings, a Rebel cannon dredged up from a river where steelworkers swam, "the shaft so close/they could have kicked it"; shot and arrowheads from the Creek village of Tallasseehatchee burned at Jackson's command. Jake Adam York's Alabama resists assimilation and simplification. In "Descendant," a grandmother cooking cornbread recounts family history, turning a skillet so her grandson can see the Hades Furnace stamp from 1843—significantly, the "year my great-great grandpa fell," pulled down "in the charge of coal." The poet is held rapt by the metal's heat, the "sweat beading" in his grandmother's hair as she works:

> But the story's gone—
> the furnace roaring, his
> falling through its molten light.
> She doesn't say a word . . .

The silent room is "filled/with the smell of roasted corn,/bread against metal" and when the cornpone's done, it falls

> hard and crusted dark
> to the plate where it steams
>
> like a heap of slag
> burnt, but whispering
> and, where she splits it,
> white.

Elsewhere, the poet acknowleged the wisdom that blood carries…

> Secrets that tell themselves
> into the static in my ear
>
> The thousand ancient signals
> just underneath the skin.

Of primary interest to York is the dynamic method by which history is forged by and through an oral tradition. *Murder Ballads* is populated by listeners: laborers who listen to the stories that metal tells, a neighbor who hears "Orion's warble" through his satellite dish, a grandmother who holds a radio close at night to hear "the dead whispering through." The poet as interferometer, then, reads the signals of multiple broadcasts: the wind playing "leaves on my ears" or Coltrane's "Alabama" raining down "like white hot iron, like stars."

Drawing on the time-honored tradition of the murder ballad, those anonymous folk songs with inevitably catastrophic narratives transplanted from the Old World and adapted to the New, Jake Adam York explores the weight of American history in terms of human victimhood and accountability. "Knoxville Girl," for instance, imagines its way into a 1956 recording by Charlie and Ira Louvin, this "the oldest song they know," an "heirloom melody" the brothers have sung since childhood, its "harmony almost gospel. // But this is not a hymn." The song's reenactment of themes inescapable in Western culture's storytelling captures the listener who already knows the immortalized, anonymous girl has

> waited years before
>
> in the Thames and the Tennessee
> for her miller, her minstrel, her country boy,
> to call her back, then strike her down
> and lay her in the stream,
>
> her hair a wild anemone,
> a millweed that snakes like flame
> to light the sheriff's page,
> an ancient tongue in guilty mouths.

Like James Wright, York knows that humanity is a kinship of "guilty mouths;" he understands, in particular, how difficult it is for us to "untangle their names from ours" ("Consolation"). Like Whitman, deeply spiritual rather than traditionally religious, he is aware of the multitudes contained within a single human soul. York refers to stories of Whitman visiting Alabama, "shaking poems from his hair/on the steps of local churches," imagining Whitman in the brief interval in which he had "begun to catch things there he had to walk off/or sing unwritten," the poet "saying his piece" before he "left the county to its mayors, its wars and local dramas." The unspoken, undocumented moments in inherited narratives interest York most: whether this poetic forebear had visited the bluff where "a hundred years thence/someone fabled a child lost from the arms/of his hispanic mother." In the changed city of the present "lit up with gasoline and beer, tremble of taillight," York reminds us, Whitman's

> . . . secrets and his song
> would be unwelcome, though he slake
> some secret thirsts, his orotund voice
> tune our ears to the river's whisper,
> a baby cradled in its branches
> deep beneath the bridge.

York, again like Wright, seeks temporary blessing in the landscape's preternatural beauty, especially its flora. In his musically and muscular verse, we find "an everywhere like fog now spoken/on our pecans' dry pouts"; "dogwood,/farkleberry, soapwart and laurel,/. . .larkspur and forget me-not—filigrees/that hold me, every step. . . ." ("Run On") Yet York is a poet who refuses to avert his eyes from darker realities that the passage of time threatens to obliterate. "From *A Field Guide to Etowah County*," reminds us that the place where "the grass does not whorl/in cursives of moonlight and dark each night," is also the place where

> . . . they found that postman
> from Baltimore, walking his integration letter
> to Ross Barnett, three hundred miles to go
> shot in head and neck, copies of the protest
> scattered and streaking in the April dew.

Fugue-like in their music and multiplicity of dimension, these poems are vigilant in their remembering. A memorial to the murder of Virgil Ware "Vigil," demonstrates York's belief in poetry as link between generations, a vehicle for a greater historical succession. The abandoned bike frame of the murdered boy must not remain fixed in time, overtaken by weeds. Instead, the poet works to transmute the specter of this literal metal frame and the memory it represents: "Let the crucible door open like a mouth," he writes

> and speak its bloom of light, molten and new.
>
> Let me stand in its halo. Let me stand
> as it pours out its stream of sun.
>
> Let me gather and hold it like a brother.
> And let it burn.

The "use of memory," Eliot warned, "is for liberation." York takes Eliot at his word. Rather than introspection, sensationalism, or mere entertainment, remembering becomes an act of engagement, one that that propels the poet toward a fierce intellectual and moral reckoning. And we in turn are held rapt by the lyric enactments of this poet who takes dangerous material into his hands; who stubbornly pulls at the poisonous sumac obscuring a steel furnace's ruins; who probes old wounds, transfiguring them into new patterns. *Murder Ballads* is wondrous and essential reading, a compelling debut.

Jane Satterfield, June 2005

MURDER BALLADS

Rehearsal to Ourselves
Of a Withdrawn Delight —
Affords a Bliss Like Murder —
Omnipotent — Acute —

We will not drop the Dirk —
Because We love the Wound
The Dirk Commemorate — Itself
Remind Us that We died —

— E.D.

I. THE BURNING MAN

Hush

It's just the wind, she says,
and not the cigarette pull
of a stranger in the roadside weeds,
the wind, and not the ember burrowing
like a mite in a dead bird's wing
or your fear that the weeds will catch
and it won't be wind any more,
the wind, and not the shadow
blazing brush toward the few
still-lit windows that glow
like cigarette tips through the leaves,
but the wind, the wind
through his hair, his lungs,
his easeful steps, quiet
as the wind or the wisteria
gripping the screen or the small boy
running through the moonlit woods
from the man who entered
like the wind in his ears
as the trellis bends
to those open, hungry hands,
or the maple shuddering at the screen
where no one's home
but the wind
that watches itself fall
to the man whose suit of flame
crackles like the wind
that comes through the screen
like a mother saying
hush it's just the wind,
or a mother saying
hush it's just the wind.

Elegy for James Knox

*Whose death, in 1924, led to the abolishment of Alabama's
convict-labor lease system.*

Because a shackle is never enough
to hold a man, but only his body,
and because the body must be made
to hold the man, to join with the chain
until the grip is overwhelming,
they took you from the prison
and sold your labor, your body
for five dollars a month, into the mine
to dig coal for Birmingham's furnaces,
the heat already pressing in on you
like a hand, the coal dust
in your lungs' own flexings
lacerating breath right out of you
little at a time, the hard pump of the arms
speeding it up in the candle-lit dark
that lay on your skin the way
they already saw you, a density
to be burned so iron could rain
from rock, purified and bright.
But to take you out, the hands
sudden from the tight, dark heat,
and beat you with a wire
spun from the kind of steel
you had begun to forge in the shaft,
to return your muscles' work this way
till you were red as ore, and then
to tie and dip you in a laundry vat
and boil the hair from your body
as if it were any pig, and then
call it *suicide*, as if you had done this
to yourself, to say you drank
bichloride of mercury instead of sweat,

instead of blood, instead of heat
and coal and *nigger*, to rule it
poison, to inject your dead body
with corrosive metal and call it
another day at the office, ready
to do it all again should the sun rise,
God willing, to ship the coal out
to charge the ironworks so someone else
could draw you from the hearth
for forging a thirty dollar check
in Mobile, and burn you into textbooks,
something dark to be turned
like this chip of iron I finger
as I think of you,
a small, hard strip of Alabama
that's losing, that's turning back
red as the clay that buries it all —
was it ever, will it ever be, enough?

Walt Whitman in Alabama

Maybe on his way to Gadsden,
Queen City of the Coosa,
to speak with the pilots and inland sailors,
to cross the fords Jackson ran with blood
or meet the mayor who
bought the ladies' favors with river quartz,
maybe east from some trip west to see
or returning north from New Orleans
or just lost in those years after The War
as legend has it, after the bannings,
when he'd grown tired of puffs and plates,
after he'd grown the beard and begun
to catch things there he had to walk off
or sing unwritten, maybe when the open road
opened on mockingbirds two and two —
no one knows, though the stories have him here
recapturing Attalla, shaking poems from his hair
on the steps of local churches. Maybe
it was the end of many letters, the last
of hospital days, another sleight
to make his hand come alive
when he couldn't bring some Southron home.
I see him there remembering his poems,
his back to the door, singing
out to the garden of the world,
the tropical spring of pine and jasmine,
how wondrous it was the pent-up river
washed to green their farms, the creeks swole
with mountain dew to sprout the corn,
herbage of poke and collard,
spinach and bean, to wash the roots
of every leaf to come. But more
I wonder what he did not say,
whether the doors were closed on the room
where none thought Jesus ever naked,
whether he went down Gadsden's Broad
to the bluff where a hundred years thence

someone fabled a child lost from the arms
of his hispanic mother and almost saved
by a cop who brought from his pocket
a shirt's worth of proof before the woman
vanished with her English, before the psychics
started rowing down the channel
to listen for the baby's dreams — all years after
the whorehouses, the fires, Reconstruction
and true religion came, after Whitman said his piece
and left the county to its mayors,
its wars and local dramas, Broad Street
and its theatres to opening and closing
and being torn down to photograph and rumor
where Vaudeville variety traveled
in those years before the world became real
and history stilled, before the dams stalled
the yearly flood that washed the roots
and made new fields from catfish and shit
and the mountain dead, before
the sun in the tassels was wormed to shine,
before shine dried into the hills
with the snakes, the poetry, the legend.
I imagine him here in the different city,
bathing in the yellow light as the river slips
beneath the bridge, flickering like a candle
or like the body or like the bodies
lit up with gasoline and beer, tremble of taillights,
while the statue of the Civil War heroine
points fingerless down Broad, down the stream
of headlamps and embers of burning weed,
a congregation in which his secrets and his song
would be unwelcome, though he slake
some secret thirsts, his orotund voice
tune our ears to the river's whisper,
a baby cradled in branches
deep beneath the bridge.
Its ribs filter the Coosa's brown.
Its arms raise the crops.
And every night it whispers the town
in some new forgotten tongue.

Knoxville Girl

(Traditional) Arranged by Charlie and Ira Louvin. Recorded May 3, 1956

The song is one their mother sang,
a campfire waltz on autumn nights
or alone, a lullaby,
the oldest song they know.

Now the tape is rolling,
Charlie on guitar, Ira mandolin,
the way they've done since they were kids,
in heirloom melody —

*I met a little girl in Knoxville,
a town we all know well —*
their voices twine, almost one,
the harmony almost gospel.

But this is not a hymn.
They walk the riverside, whittling
smooth that driftwood branch
they'll use to *strike that fair girl down*

where she'll plead for mercy,
dark eyes twinkling
like the river in the wind
as they *only beat her more.*

They'll grab her *by her golden curls*
and *drag her round and round,*
and *throw her into the river*
that runs through Knoxville town.

8

In the song, they never pause
but run on home to bed and dream
her singing hush-now rhymes
while the sheriff fiddles at the door

and we never see her raised
from the stream's thick water.
But the song is old,
and she has waited years before

in the Thames and the Tennessee
for her miller, her minstrel, her country boy
to call her back, then strike her down
and lay her in the stream,

her hair a wild anemone,
a millweed that snakes like flame
to light the sheriff's page,
an ancient tongue in guilty mouths

or moonlight through the bars
of the cinder-block *cell*
where they sit for *killing that Knoxville girl,*
that girl they *loved so well.*

Sweat gleams on the guitar's face.
Ira holds the chord in the mandolin
till the wood is still.
They wait as the tape rolls out,

smoothing like a stream to hold
sky's last light,
till she's still and quiet
as a lullaby child.

On Tallasseehatchee Creek

In November 1813, Andrew Jackson sent 1,000 men to destroy
the village of Tallasseehatchee, killing nearly 200 of the 300
Creeks living there by burning them in their homes.

Clear till it hits the bend
where we work the village
out of clay, where post-molds graph
the longhouses' outlines in ash

we broke through days ago.
Inside the lines, the ground is smooth
with the fat of those
who burned alive, the man who pulled

himself into the fire, gunshot legs
behind, the woman Crockett said
strung arrows with her feet.
Tomorrow, we should hit the cellars

whose cooked potatoes the soldiers ate
once the ashes cooled,
maybe some cache of bones or greasy tubers,
something to confirm the tale,

though nothing's strong enough to keep
the earthmovers from moving in.
In a month, the bank becomes the angle
of Azalea Dogleg, the creek

gives up its name to Hazard
and the town's elusive grammar,
the *village captured by the stream*
turns under fertilized greens.

Here, where the water darkens, red,
where we sift the earth for sherds,
I wash an arrowhead
into the sun's steel-white gleam,

then sieve fists of rock through my hands
till I finger something strange —
a tiny ball of polished iron,
shot distilled from clay.

When the chief sends me back
for metal detectors and finer screens,
I thread in quiet the subdivision maze
of streets already named,

Arrowhead Drive, Ember Lane.

Looking for Cane Creek Furnace

Calhoun County, Alabama

Where by all accounts it should have been,
a stone millhouse without a wheel,
its grindstones strewn about the woods,
the creek, and the army's fence,
the army's ditch and razor wire
that keep us from the weapons dump,
chemical igloos
gleaming bright as molten iron.
Cold chain link scalds our hands
as we scan that frozen village
for the stone foundation's jags,
where slag would crackle underfoot
and you could touch the smooth hearth floor
where the *Merrimac*'s plates were forged.
But the signs all say it's death
till after we are dead and gone.

We turn as smoke gathers in the branches
then scatters like crows
when the millhouse windows catch the sun.
When the glare fades
the man and his wife are fighting.
She pleads as he lands the answers
that rock her like shells
on the range beyond the hill.
When he turns to stoke the fire,
their faces catch the glow.
The fire slides down her cheeks.
And here the wind plays leaves on my ears,
crackle of water arguing with stone
or ice underfoot, as overhead the trees
shiver quicker in the rising heat.

Cannon

They bring it up in chains,
rusted dark as mud,
and the bore shoots water
till right. The whole crowd scatters,
convinced it's charged.
Scientists wave it over, unalarmed.
A whistle blows, and a shift
of steelworkers turns from the river,
amazed the Rebel cannon lay
so close, just feet below
when they swam, slow nights,
the water hot, metallic,
iron biting at their tongues,
so close they could have kicked it.
At dark, blue flame
rises from the gas-plant,
painting everything with its glow,
and the furnace crew perches
to watch the river steam.
One by one, they rise
to trawl the bank, tracing
exhausts upstream and down.
The others slump on the rails,
still warm, like the test-irons
they worry in their hands,
thinking how the metal smells,
how dear it holds
whatever heat you give.

Descendant

She flips the skillet
so I'll read the stamp —
Hades Furnace,
1843 —

then turns, explaining,
Year my great-great grandpa fell,
then feeds the skillet
to the oven, heat

raising wisps of hair.
Now the meal is sifted,
she says, *My grandma said*
he never left

without his cornbread,
then tips the buttermilk in,
and even when he didn't show,
whisking till it blends,

his bread was waiting —
even when the master came,
saying how he'd fell,
pulled down in the charge of coal.

The air is acrid, metal,
as she draws the skillet
and pours the batter,
crackling, white,

then feeds it to the oven
once again, then stands,
hands in apron,
sweat beading in her hair.

But the story's gone —
the furnace roaring, his
falling through its molten light.
She doesn't say a word.

When the room is filled
with the smell of roasted corn,
bread against metal,
she stands, a towel in her hand,

then draws and flips the skillet
so the cornpone falls,
hard and crusted dark
to the plate where it steams

like a heap of slag,
burnt, but whispering
and, where she splits it,
white.

Midnight, Furnace, Wind

Halfway through the second heat, we see him shouting
from the floor, something to say. Always something to say.
He said the metal had stories to tell, said
he heard them whispering when he tapped the iron.
Heat, he'd say, *is just the same goods moving —*
iron just mountain running fast as rivers cut it,
its ore, coal, and bone now quick as tongues.
Now he's running, arms waving, still shouting,
face turning red, but you can't hear a thing.
Can't tell the Bessemers' blowing from the wind
or the hiss of quenched steel or the rinse
someone forgot exploding under molten iron
in the ladle overhead. But we see the sunrise glow
spreading on his face, his mouth brightening
as if those tongues flickered there, and then
the metal cauling him, a man of fire, walking, then
reaching out, then gone.

                                            One night,
when the blast sparks swarmed like yellowjackets,
I breathed one in, coughed back a sphere of metal
still cooling in a whisper of spit. That was all we found,
beads that rolled for the drains, and a quiet
that held for weeks, steam hiss scattering everyone.
I'd sit, the foremen yelling in my radio, remembering
his face, bathed in light, something like a smile
curling there, the way he cocked his head as if to listen
to the burn. The sort of thing we should have heard.
It sounds like the spaces between the yelling,
a little squelch then static waiting to be broken,
like his open empty mouth, like watching him shout
and hearing nothing but the rush,
everyone deaf to what the metal said.

Breakfast

He sits, shirtless, still, as she digs the steel
from the cauterized wound. Morning
flashes off the knife. He doesn't say a word.

Not *graveyard*. Not *lucky*. How iron
reaches out for iron. He keeps his quiet
as she cuts the barb of night from his arm.

As morning combs his hair, molten light
burning through the grey his father left
in photos he's grown into, one by one.

Steam curls where bacon rusts our eggs.
The radio whispers between the same old songs.
How the metal can't stay still.

I fist my knife as she twists the blade.
A flash. A flash. I turn away.

II. INTERFERENCE

. . . meaning

What words mean when they are given
From so many voices, I do not know myself
Who is speaking and who is listening.

— Rodney Jones

Interferometry

The dish,
           like a moon on my neighbor's roof,
gathers light

though it isn't light he's after,

no football or satellite films,
but the sound of light
                      instead.

Last week he called me over
to listen to Orion's warble,

the stars' ancient waves
twinkling in and out
                      through the solar wind,

caught clear as local channels
in his homemade radio.

The dish wanes tonight,
                      maybe searching
for more exotic noise,

black holes or planets cutting in,

and I try to hear, holding still,
the night's music in his basement room

but can't break through.

As I shift in my sweat
                      the dish waxes full
and the crickets'

high and quickening cycle

                    rises

like so many stars

sunk in the grass and burning,
burning the night
                with song.

Blew

Cornflower blue, blue
as moonlight on the hand,

a well in the hay
where light lies down,

a child, the boy
lies like a shadow,

blue as newborn,
but quieter. But quiet.

His trim fingers tremble
the reeds — or the reeds

tremble them — till still
where midnight stitches

every gleam,
stalk and skin skeined down,

as dark takes hold.
Rustle combs the field

and, caught,
ripe grass lavishes

seed-head and tassel,
fine braids with fine,

moonlit and indigo, crow,
the urgent edge with cool.

And the cornflower,
the stray weed's calyx

bends to the down
and dew-wet brow

its cerulean creel
to weir the glacial bright

where his skin gives way
that gives way where

the stars weld their love
on the nights in his eyes.

Those patient flames —
do they know? —

they have hours.
They will never close.

And from such hearths
can they see

the constellations crowding
deep in his crepuscular gasp,

stealing luster from the tongue
and those slowly drying oxbows,

his lips? Or those last,
bluest leaves of the flower

that winds down the breath
that wants only wind?

Or the flower, slowly closing
like a word

that can only dream
of a blooming, a wind,

an ear?

Fell

The map of heaven fades
beneath the levee,

its stars swallowed
in the slag's obsidian coils,

Draco wrestling
moccasin and magnolia

till all eyes cinder,
its sulphurous whispers drown.

Twilight holds,
stoked by the furnace

and the gas-plant's flame,
and the last coals

twinkle through the heaps
to the river's scroll.

•

When midnight breaks the levee
the map is gone

and every fall's
a crest catching moon,

a second's etch from dark to dark
that ends in iron.

Then the channel whites,
a meteor's burn

withering to the snake
that haunts the pumice shoals,

striking every eddy dead
till it mounts the slag,

its head arrowing through
the stranger's smoldering wings,

its length, a mantle
on his shoulders,

black and scabbed with stars,
risen for this last tattoo.

George Wallace at the Crossroads

*After losing the 1958 Alabama Democratic Gubernatorial
Primary, Wallace is said to have disappeared for a month,
returning to declare that he'd "never be out-niggered again."*

No guitar. Just the one, quivering string.
Abnegated gut begun to hate itself.
The throat's weary chords, his hands.

I enter by whiskey, set to
work, retune the flesh.
My favorite music rises.

Everything I touch holds the song
already. The fallen star's
swallowed question. Hot night wind.

This body's never quiet.
It sings like a fire.
As he walks off, toward Montgomery,

they fall again. The whole state
burns in the light.

Radiotherapy

Because they lived near the signal tower,
voltage purring like a church
before the preacher starts,
or because she's talking
in the very middle of the noise,
the doctor says to pray,
to radiate The Word of God into the boy
and recall each fallen cell
to the righteous body. But all he hears
is grandma's story, how at night,
if you hold your radio close
you can hear the dead whispering through.
She explains how her sisters
wired their mom's old Silvertone
after she had passed away,
braiding her hair in the speaker's leads.
She says that if he listens
he can hear her sisters arguing
over every static's peak, her mother
saying *Time for bed.*
When she starts again,
in the distance, someone's asking
why it won't stop hurting,
and the church is working like a round,
everyone trying to start
something new.
But all anyone can say
is what they've said before,
old stories, old prayers
all that's breaking through.

What You Wish For

Wind is the only braid for miles.
    Then you descend to the river.
Mud and catfish stench twine in your hair,
    the only waves. No nightjar
or solitary oar, but you imagine
    a kid, laid deep in a thicket
guitaring to the stars and his lonely girl,
    an open window miles away.
A wisp of melody, a radio
    wide awake in an empty house.
Something you always wanted her
    to hear. Maybe the hum of *the body*
under her hands, just rising *from the water,*
    someone to whisper in your ear
before sunrise, like this voice you imagine
    from faint notes of wind. *Sources*
say a tooth, silver and quicksilver filled,
    can unfold radio, the skull
like a guitar's face amplifies vibration
    into your backseat darling. So perhaps
this girl, *missing now since Tuesday,*
    or the girl in mind, perhaps this voice
is nothing you imagine, but a drift,
    a weather grown audible
in the charge of your jaw. A report,
    an echo. *A fisherman working,*
every grapple down, *beneath the bridge*
    raised the body of, an echo,
this poor half-amputated girl, *her arms,*
    the tongue cut from her throat
raised from the waveless stream,
    whose voice is lost in the forest
on the snag of a sweetgum tree.
    You imagine the kid, awaiting
this hung reply, a wail gone *out walking*
    after midnight, searching for him.

It *walks for miles, along the highway,*
   but that's just her way of saying
I Love You. The news is gone. The notes
   thrill, a pulse in solid bone.
Or you imagine none of this
   and no station you can raise
plays this tune. But you hope
   you don't know this any other way,
you search the car for a strip of foil,
   chewing gum or cigarette tin,
and grind it down between your teeth
   and your prayer for a spark
and the acrid pain to fill your mouth,
   to make these voices all go away.

Blood

One cell reaching out,
two cells talking.

Then, what they keep on saying
and the silence in between.

A syntax of organs.
A rumor the body shares.

Twist, little ribbon.
Keep coming undone.

Petal, rust,
fingerprint felt.

Secrets that tell themselves
into the static in my ear.

The thousand ancient signals
just underneath the skin.

Run On

An everywhere like fog now spoken
    on our pecans' dry pouts

the matin rises, note to chord.
    Ascent's legatos congregate

our waking. *What comfort this*
    sweet sentence gives. Hallelujahs

wren in the thinning grove, distance
    coming to. *Shout on, pray on,*

we're gaining ground. I offer my ease,
    my quiet to each grasp

in this careful mounting — dogwood,
    farkleberry, soapwort and laurel,

to larkspur and forget-me-not — filigrees
    that hold me, every step,

and the lost is found where kudzu parts,
    pine shafts truss

its woven night and now it fails
    where nature all in ruin lies,

where — *Great God stop* — the chapel gleams
    with the morning of *the midnight dews,*

and while the river skips its harp
    the valley long, it will not refuse

the other shore — *Go tell that long-time liar,*
    go tell that midnight rider —

and the man, playing his shadow right in time,
    singing *Run on for a long time,*

Run 'long for a long time, God a mighty,
    just a-wailing on his self,

his *self—Great God—*knocking it open
    like it was made of dawn.

Bunk Richardson

Lynching photograph: February 11, 1906: Gadsden, Alabama

The rope grips the iron
where the iron bites into its hold.
A noose of rust, dried blood.

The dew has frozen in its twines,
thicker near the river,
from which it's climbed

weaker and weaker, all night long.

Under

The water scars, blade
and keel
          Oars
                    the rotors' pulse
blade down
                    bleeds down.
When it dies
                    I can break

from the silt's thick hands
                              to raise
a scent for hounds
                         and rise without fear
from the clench of rock
and bone
                    but water
don't work that way,
                         the river
holds its tributes
speaking like the drowned.

When the surface
                    hushes
heals
          the chain iron's
rattling
          I kick from the mud
and pull
               growing lung,
                              where
torches
          rope and chain
break the water's skin,
flickering rendezvous
                    the rowboat

35

waiting,
         my conductor
                        the sheriff
and his boys
              putting

things the water's
                   pulling in.

Doppler

His sleep like arms enfolds
the boy, blue-hole blue
easy not to harm his sleep
while the other arms braced
for a moment that wouldn't happen.
No father in the door.
Just a wall made of mumbling
and t.v. And then an attic room
so floored. If he didn't hear them
flipping *Jeopardy, Touched by An Angel,*
he'd curl into the tick, but this
was not the usual shack with him
in the icehouse off the kitchen.
I had seen it weeks before
when the one was trying
to fish his son from the river
at Stockholm Bend while the other
broke his chain gang
for a vise and a map of Florida.
He could smell me in the attic
but told himself he had
someone else in mind. When
are they going to do something?
His arms like water enfold me.
He holds a king and two jacks,
one he calls a knave. He draws
his house then passes me a beer.
I know blue-hole blue cut open
would shine like clay, but the boy
bleeds like a thermometer
I can drink against my pocket's weathers.
So I said not the usual shack.
In the icehouse off the kitchen
I can't hear any of this.
Just a game show and the embrace

of beer cans on knees. Why
do they wait? Do they wait? I told him
I was grabbing catfish, my arm
through a hole in my rotten boat
when I saw the camphouse and knew
my daddy wouldn't take me.
So I drowned. That boy
never did listen. Listen: I drowned
him then hid in the attic
to wait for you. I smelled myself
but had someone else in mind.
I was on the bank poling for my drowned.
I was watching through the murk.
When I reached through the window,
I was in the next room waiting
for someone to do it. I agreed
to bury the coins by the stump
and was later asked to dig them up.
The others waited in the fringe,
arms itching with empty.
When I went over the bluff
I was waiting in the cove
with a six-pack and
a jar of silver dollars. The boat
was made from a Florida map
and for oars we used a criminal
and my dad's remote control.

Double Exposure

Not even a father yet
my grandfather leans against
the grille of his '46 Packard,
new chrome blinding

even in black-and-white.
His white slacks billow
like a skirt in the wind.
His hair is perfectly still.

The war is behind him.
The road winds up from the farm.
One cornhusk hand
slips from the fender

and into the fingers
that ghost his fingers,
the thin, delicate lace
that haunts his hems.

The more I look, the more
he looks like someone else,
ringlets massing in his hair,
the gaze gone strangely tender,

the smile now doubly bright —
bright as the rings on his finger
casting what they cannot hold,
as if ready to part, to say

what's hidden's never hid
but beating like a second heart,
a second pulse in the pulse
that runs through everything.

From *A Field Guide to Etowah County*

Bluets, larkspur, common violets in the jimson
and queen-anne's-lace, tangles of boxwood
and honeysuckle and smilax in hydrangea and pine,
thick from which Spring Azures drift,
among the first to emerge, then Swallowtails'
gunmetal iridescence, obsidian-with-stars
wings turning like pages in hands of wind.
Thrashers tear in the leaves for earthworms,
salamanders, some morsel, their stipple
of sunlight-in-leaves blending then reappearing
in a crash of meal. If a snake uncurls,
the bird will leaf it in bibles of territory, protection,
and someone's aunt or grandmother, passing,
will slow to note that summer is on us early.
But this one merely stands, its wing in a ray,
feathers a concrete mottle of grain and pebble
like a roadside table turned into brush long ago.
Here, there is no cankered plum or split persimmon,
sap or juice to bead, mimeograph bright,
on the grass's nibs, and the grass does not whorl
in cursives of moonlight and dark each night,
but this is where they found that postman
from Baltimore, walking his integration letter
to Ross Barnett, three hundred miles to go,
shot in his head and neck, copies of the protest
scattered and streaking in the April dew.
It was September, honeysuckle in full perfume,
the woods a riot of grackles and jays,
when the grand jury broke and let the suspect go.
The facts are simple, my grandfather said,
the D. A. said we couldn't make a case,
so the words they never wrote coiled
in field reports and requisitions, and three days later
a church-bomb in Birmingham

blew the stained-glass face of Christ
like a dandelion head in the roadside weeds.
Snakeroot, aster, and blazing star, some
toxic to cows, should not be eaten, though many take
the greens and fruit of poke, more abundant
in Spring, as correctives, small poisons
to set things right. Goldenrod blazes the highway's
shoulders, all the way to Birmingham
or Chattanooga, and starlings gather
like glass, like grackles in the trees, such
sociability an advance of colder weather.
The Swallowtails and Azures have disappeared,
but you may spot the Great Purple Hairstreak
bumbling, slow and easy to observe,
even in the clouds of goldenrod that dust
when they land. The cones are brilliant
but delicate as their gossamer wings. Touch,
and the color's written in your skin.

For Viola Liuzzo

Selma to Montgomery,
fifty miles. The only signs

for Trickem, White Hall.
Tallawassee Creek.

And somewhere, the imprint
in the shoulder, the shadow

where you came to rest,
gunned down and left

where the pines encroach.
A mark someone could show.

It's March again.
Traffic wakes the grass.

But the road, it keeps
its quiet. Fifty miles

and not a sign
but the FBI's

fifteen hundred pages,
but the crosses and weeds

and these tender creeping violets,
slow confederates winking

through the thatch, trying hard
to keep from being overcome.

Elegy for Little Girls

Sloss Furnaces, Birmingham, September 16th, 1963

Puncture the mud, the iron pours out

•

tongue of fire, not a word

•

stays still but breaks along the channels

•

pressed in the cast floor's sand.

•

Now it's pigs suckling at the sow's

•

iron teats, so many children blind

•

to the air and world that harden them.

•

A gift. Dark come on. When

•

the slag-man pulls the plug, fire

•

explodes, its violent, molten light

•

bathes the irons, a glow on their spines

•

like stained glass or twilight fades

•

on headstones' crests, row on row on row

Notes Toward an Elegy

The waxwings return
    now the mockingbird's distracted
to poach from the elaeagnus
    its fat berries set
in thorns like eyes
    boned from human hands

while in the distance
    a woman stops her car
and biers something in tissues
    from the road, lays it
in the crepe myrtles
    at the curb, a bundle

I later see, a waxwing
    folded on itself forever,
the tips of its secondaries
    a primary red,
its mask even more a mystery
    now there's nothing left

to find, nothing of the mastery
    of air or unminded skill
in picking insect from air
    or nesting straw from vine,
from vine the berry, every-
    thing handled by the grasp

of bone and beak, the beaks
    still working just yards away
as if unmindful, or as if they
    can only keep moving
with their contraction of hand
    and mouth, their one cry.

III. AS WATER

I looked down from great height
at a burned world I believed
I never had to enter.

— Philip Levine

As Water

near Climax, Colorado
the Continental Divide

My washed hands steam
like the peaks after rain.
The vapors drift

like the dirt, a cloud of lead
and iron and gold
in the stream's clear weather.

•

As the sunflower
answers the sun.

Translates radiance
to seed and oil.

Alloys it makes
of earth and sky.

Gold bees wing.

•

47

Over the Platte, the Wind,
the Republican River's turns.
Columbine and timothy.

Monkshood, yucca, pasque.
Canyongrass and locoweed
and quarterback

•

gnawing gingerroot
deep in the grain
till he can't be smelled,

breathing through woodsmoke,
through campfires and hearth-smell
and barbecues starting on tomorrow

the scent of hung meat sweating,
fat-ash, skin,
the muscle fallen to the coal.

•

In Beaumont, the hanged man's body,
burnt crisp, beyond.

In Tulsa, the black homes burning,
the gunpowder wind.

In Sioux Falls and Salinas, the stench
of birch and blood and hide,
the great still staring

that bring the nightsweats on,
twitch and gnash, moans
hung like a haze of sodium light

•

flowering anvil-clouds
over Missouri
and Arkansas and Tennessee,

over Jackson and Nashville
and Birmingham, Atlanta,
over boredom and afternoon breaking

from Scottsboro to Bristol,
from Memphis to Augusta,
then washing west

•

drawing shot-iron and arrowheads
from the hills, bone
and blood that twine

with the float of gold-dust
and lead that washes through Gadsden
and Ohatchee, through Horseshoe Bend
and Montgomery and Selma
and Camden and Mobile

where the nightsweats run
to the river and under the bridge,
and whole towns shiver

•

as I raise my smoking hands
in moonlight
a thousand miles away

and watch them burn.

IV. CONSOLATION

In the Magic City

Birmingham

The needle floats over and over
    the end of Coltrane's "Alabama,"
channeling in the rush of feet,
    of tires wearing down
into the asphalt and the browning air
    the static that backs the horn

when I start it up again.
    Tyner almost sweats
what he keeps just out of time,
    what Jimmy's talking from the strings
like something's coiled up there,
    a static even Elvin never shakes.

Or maybe what the needle thinks,
    some Old South air trapped in ladled steel,
a space that quotes the ridges
    and their empty veins, old Sloss
filling up with fire
    or Cherry's heat opening 16th Street

into the space Coltrane fills
    when he feeds his tenor,
what Sun Ra kept opening out
    for anything more
than George Wallace's crossroads deal,
    the static in Clifford Gibson singing

Keep your windows pinned
    as storm winds thrill Sloss's tunnels
and flush its ghosts out over the city
    where Vulcan's torch goes red,
Coltrane raining down his "Alabama"
    like white-hot iron, like stars

that draw from the dark as they spin
    Maubilla and Horseshoe Bend
the way Elvin works the cymbals
    into distant crowds.

And when it ends again
    I step out and through the blocks
where you can hear
    the quartets warming up
through the nightclub chatter
    and hope tonight,

in one of these joints
    some DJ breaks all his needles,
some combo plays harder
    than they've ever played,
that someone, that anyone
    will work just hard enough

to shut the city down
    and groove the night again.

Janney

Ohatchee, Alabama

Hidden like a sentry,
the furnace blooms
with sumac, crawls with lizards.
It smokes off rain so hard

you can hear them breathe,
one breath lifting granite,
pulling coal, the hundred hands
digging wells in the hill

where the forge-works rust,
above, where their graves
hoard irons all their own
and take on water just in case.

From there, I could jump
to the stack's jagged rim
and stare down the barrel
to this crossroads of light

and fable a blast or
count saplings to predict its fall.
But here, where the tuyeres draw wind
to spin the rumor of fire

and the crucible sings like a shell
the edge seems years away.
The smoke never clears.
The stones stay warm to the touch.

Maybe, if rain could wake the Coosa
to flood this wild, to roll
the stone beneath the slag and clay again,
maybe then, we'd have a chance.

But the clouds move on.
The thunder's gone to Georgia.
A mud bloom cools
in the hearth's debris

and a copperhead coils from the brash,
bright as molten iron.
I ease back, and breathe,
grasping at sumacs,

ready to turn and run.
And when I do I pull
to feel them give,
to feel their blisters break.

At Cornwall Furnace

Cherokee County, Alabama

Blown out just after The War.
The stack's granite gapes. Each year
saplings try, as gravity has
longer, a reclamation masonry won't allow.
Lichens and moss do more.

Promises of love and forevers
mural its inside
above constellations of beer cans and glass,
ashes. The lid of sky's diameter
remains the same.

In water only yards away,
confluence of the Coosa and Chatooga,
mud ebbs from a bed of scoria,
slag I can find in channels
miles south. Algae homes in its pocks.

The friend who has brought me here
stands waist-deep in the rivers,
taking pictures
near a deadwood stump
when her feet find something odd.

Together we struggle from the water
a mass of pig-iron the size of a liver.
It's why Noble's men built it.
Probably a product of the last blast.
Too late. We can imagine

the boys who mined and cut the rock,
brought the hematite, ore, and limestone,
the slaves

sweating in their tunnel under the hill,
but do not. We know what fire

will burn here tonight, what
fumes will rise.
Flawless architecture of a monument.
Silent,
we heft the pig and give it back.

Negatives

Townspeople gathered for the burning of John Lee. August 13, 1911, Durant, Oklahoma. Gelatin silver print. Real photo postcard. 5"x 3"

You cannot see the body
each eye fixes, the focus

of the plume that angles every head,
John Lee, curling skyward

from the fire,
a town's worth of bullets

searing white in the char
that was a man, gunned down

and set ablaze. John Lee
will burn till sundown,

till ash and *a few charred parcels*,
till the crowd disbands and spreads

to the corners of the town
now shut of every black,

and poor Miss Campbell's *poor white soul*
drifts, *avenged*, to heaven

till the photographer bends to his film
to darken the postcard caption,

block letters that will blaze white
COON COOKING — the *barbecue*

one will later describe
on the opposite side. But for now

you can see only smoke
and the appetite on the faces

closest to the heat,
the desperate arching of a body

eager for a glimpse of the gravity,
the magnetism of this powerless man.

But let us imagine
just afterward, the camera slung

on the taker's shoulder,
and at its heart a thousand blacks

staring into this cloud of light,
for a moment neither

gathering toward nor
descending from heaven,

but waiting in their adoration
and blessing each with its glow —

a vision of these thousand whites
turned dark for an hour

and praying, terrified, to this pillar
for the rectifying light

and then imagine,
their prayer, the paper

slowly darkening in the light
until they are restored, white from dark,

but the cloud now a dark tornado
caught on the verge of breaking through,

ready to consume each watcher
until all there is is this plume,

the body enlarged,

its ash, a thousand postcards
of a world he dared not dream he dreamed,

signed with the names of all who watch,
ready to inscribe the scene

Wish you were here.

Vigil

The bike, the handlebars, the fork,
spoked wheels still spinning off sun,

still letting go his weight as he
lay in the grass along Docena Road

just hours after the bomb went off
under the church steps downtown,

four girls dead, though they hadn't heard,
Virgil with a bullet in his heart, Virgil Ware

who wanted a bike for a paper-route
who perched on his brother's handlebars

and caught the white boys' bullet
but never got a bike or a headstone

or a 14th birthday, Virgil and his brother
and the bike in the grass off Docena Road.

The handlebars, fork, and iron diamond
frame that held them both, warming

in the Alabama sun. Stars of paint and chrome
that rained all over north Birmingham,

up and down the Docena–Sandusky road,
nesting like crickets in the weeds.

And the seat, wearing at the edges,
the cushion opening like a cattail

to the wind. But the frame still holding,
to be handed down and down and down

till bright as a canna. Then laid
with its brothers in a tangle in the sun.

Then gathering heat and darkening.
Then weeds insinuating the fork,

the sprocket, the pedal, each iron artery,
working back toward the light.

Let their flowers open from the mouths
of the handlebars and the seat-post.

Let them be gathered from the frame
and the frame raised up. Let it be

hot to the touch. Let its rust burn
into the finest creases of the hand

and the warp of the shirtsleeve and the pants
and worked into the temples' sweat.

Then let it descend into the furnace like a hand
that opens all its rivers, each tribute,

each channel, each buried town.
Let it gather this heat, this fire, hold it all.

Let the crucible door open like a mouth
and speak its bloom of light, molten and new.

Let me stand in its halo. Let me stand
as it pours out its stream of suns.

Let me gather and hold it like a brother.
And let it burn.

Consolation

for Willie Edwards, Jr.,
murdered January 23, 1957
outside Montgomery, Alabama

If we could take them back,
swinging by the Little Kitchen's shadow
on Jefferson Street and waving them in
as they were, Livingston, Alexander,
Britt, and York, piling together
on the back bench seat of some Rambler
or Packard or 56 Chevy we've found
just to take them back, maybe
Boyett, too, maybe Boyett
in front, beside the wheel, cruising up
Ripley and Traction Streets
to Lower Wetumpka Road, past
the tangle of railroad but not quite
to Chisolm, if we could be waiting
in a semi by the road writing
this poem by a pen-light and waiting
for Livingston to come with his gun
and pull us out and take us back
to the idling car, if we could
not look at each other until
the door closes out the moon,
till the car starts cruising west
back through the railyards, maybe
catching Race Street to give the boys
one last tasteless laugh before
turning north along the L&N,
if we could take some comfort
in the pulse of the cylinders
that will pull us to 100
before they'll notice, if we could
take their punches and gibes

and maybe cry and beg for mercy
just to take them back,
and not let up when we turn
onto old 143 toward the river,
feeling the gentle tug of the engine
along this levee of road and maybe just
catch a wink from each other
in the rearview as the moon
clears the trees, then lay the needle down
gunning through the barricades
and ROAD CLOSED signs
and up the amputated ramp
where the bridge should be,
the bridge where you stood
that January night, 1957,
a gun in your side, knowing
you didn't do a thing, knowing
the river gives more than a gun, knowing
how cold and hard the water's
going to hit, if we could see them
seeing the bridge is missing,
feel them feeling this terrible pull,
if we could take them down, untangle
their names from ours, maybe
we could, a minute, rejoice
that no one will ever fall
from this height again, no one
will tangle three months in the river
and be raised up anonymous
and accidental, maybe
we will swim from the wreck
as no one drowns and stand
from the water inside our names,
our names ours at last, this poem
in our pockets like a charm
we turn as we walk home again
gleaming in the delicate light
of the bright, unfalling stars.

Release

1934

Lomax slides the record
from its sleeve, eases the needle
down. Governor sits,
quiet, till the voice unwinds

Irene, goodnight, Irene, goodnight
and then he leans,
one wing-tip tapping out the chords,
Goodnight, Irene, Goodnight, Irene.

Lomax pulls the door behind,
leaves Leadbelly pleading on,
Sometimes I had a great notion
to jump in the river and drown,

already down the hall by the time
Leadbelly moans,
If Irene turns her back on me,
I'm gonna take morphine and die.

Governor sits, the needle riding
the smooth, central quiet,
a cycle sure as chain-gang hammers,
a father singing sisters back to sleep,

I'll see you in my dreams,
the violence in the sweetest things.
He starts the record over and calls
for the papers, dreaming

Leadbelly cradling the 12-string
in his cell. It's July
in Louisiana.
The ink never dries.

Iron

I thought we all began with air,
everything in debt to oxygen
or water, the air locked there.
But today the papers say iron:

this world's first life
breathed iron in
and blew air out.
Then came all the rest.

Now my yard will never look the same,
the deep rust of clay
flashing through the scrub,
old ocean floor, ash of air.

It shines like the bank of native ochre
that's piled across the road
to shoulder rails like favorite sons
and give to the grip of trailer-kids

who mine the bank
for a clod to open like an apple,
then charged with the shock of iron
run the tracks and play grenades.

When they eat I wonder
what they see,
what I saw
before my parents straightened me

with talk of kind.
The simple dirt, or fruit without tree?
Today, they scale the levee
as thunderheads swell,

and as I cross the road
and clamber to the gravel bed,
the taste rises, familiar as lipstick,
a ghost on my tongue.

The distance rumbles in.
We can smell the coming storm.
But I'll stride the rails a minute longer,
then bend beside the kids,

fill my hands
and begin again,

right here.